Wakanda forever
Wakanda historical book
Incwadi yembali kaWakanda

Adeola pelumi

Table of Contents

Chapter 1:

History: World of Wakandan (Ilizwe laseWakandan)

Wakanda is an imaginary country in East Africa. It is situated in sub-Saharan Africa and is home to the superhuman Dark Jaguar. Wakanda previously showed up in Fabulous Four (July 1966) and was made by Stan Lee and Jack Kirby
Wakanda has shown up in comics and different media variations, like in the Wonder Realistic Universe, where it is portrayed as the most mechanically progressed country on earth.

Wakanda is found only north of Lake Turkana, at a point lining Kenya, Ethiopia, Uganda, and South Sudan.
A few sources place Wakanda only north of Tanzania and precisely at Rwanda, while others - like the Wonder Chart book - show it at the north finish of Lake, in the middle of between South Sudan, Uganda, Kenya, and Ethiopia (and encompassed by fictitious nations like Azania, Canaan, and Nairobi).
Chief Ryan Coogler expressed that his portrayal of Wakanda in the 2018 film Dark Puma was propelled by the Southern African Realm of Lesotho.
Wakanda is situated on Lake Victoria, close to individual fictitious countries Mohannda, Canaan, Azania, and Niganda.

This places these countries for the most part in what, in actuality, is the eastern portion of the Vote-based Republic of the Congo.
Birnin Zana is situated inside Wakanda. Being a shrewd city is viewed by some. In Birnin Zana, people on foot stroll along business-filled roads that are sans vehicles except for a periodic appearance of (buslike) transports.

The entire is very like the woonerf idea, a way to deal with the public space plan that began in the Netherlands during the 1970s. Maglev trains are seen speeding above and around the city. The Wakandan structures integrate a few customary African components (for example covered rooftops and hanging gardens) on probably the tallest designs.

Wakanda, formally known as the Realm of Wakanda, is a little country in upper east Africa. For quite a long time they stayed in separation from the world's local area. However, since laying out political relations with the remainder of the globe, they are presently viewed as the most innovatively progressed country on earth. The seat of government and the Regal Royal residence is situated in the capital city of Birnin Zana.

The significant dialects spoken in Wakanda are Wakandan, Yoruba, and Hausa. As a result of their high-level schooling system, however, Wakandans likewise talk a few African and European dialects, including English, German, and Latin.

Wakanda is wealthy in regular assets, including coal, oil, uranium, and precious stones. In any case, notwithstanding having the absolute biggest oil stores on the planet, the nation doesn't try to extricate them All things considered, they depend on elective energy sources, for example, sun-oriented and hydrogen. To stay away from the "Dutch sickness," the Wakandans enhanced their abundance by putting resources into arising economies. At present, they have public stores identical to trillions of U.S. dollars.

The country's most important normal asset and the hotspot for the vast majority of its mechanical advances are Wakandan Vibranium. This sort of Vibranium, found exclusively in Wakanda, can assimilate vibratory or motor energy, making it extremely challenging to annihilate. Vibranium is sold for $10,000 per gram. Wakanda's holy hill is assessed to have around 10,000 metric lots of the material, making the country's Vibranium assets alone worth roughly a quadrillion dollars.

Wakandans have generally been the most progressive country on earth in science and innovation. Their researchers envisioned the molecule an entire century sooner than Western researchers, and they have grown almost unhackable PC frameworks. They've likewise fostered a high-level, Vibranium-based interchanges innovation called Kimoyo Dots, which are worn like a wristband. The dabs can be utilized to follow an individual's well-being,

Wakanda is a high-level military power with an imposing armed force, naval force, and air monitor. Throughout the long term, Wakanda has been gone after by French, English, Belgian, and Islamic trespassers, yet in its whole history, the country has never been caught by adversary powers. The Wakandans likewise have broad knowledge assets that have been depicted as being "comparable to the Mossad" and "unquestionably better than the C.I.A."

The Wakandan strict framework depends on factions attached to African divine beings known as the Ennead. The strict customs incorporate the Hyena Group, Crocodile Clique, Lion Religion, the now prohibited White Gorilla Faction, and the Puma Faction. The Jaguar Clique is the state religion of Wakanda.

The lord and regal group of Wakanda are safeguarded by a gathering of female guardians known as the Dora Milaje ("revered ones"). Initially, the Dora Milaje were taken from each clan and thought of as likely sovereigns for an unmarried ruler. Today, they are profoundly prepared security specialists — a cross between U.S. Secret Assistance specialists and the Naval force SEALs.

Albeit the imperial genealogy is genetic, to become a ruler an individual needs to finish a progression of assessments that are challenging to the point that main up-and-comers who have had extraordinary preparation from youth can qualify. However, regardless of being an outright government, the Wakandans have a meritocratic way to deal with eminence. One time per year, there's a daily when any Wakandan can challenge the lord for a high position. Some portion of the test incorporates outclassing the ruler in a single hand-to-hand battle.

The ongoing lord of Wakanda is T'Challa, the child of T'Chaka. T'Challa isn't the main leader of the realm yet additionally top of the profoundly based hero religion, known as the Jaguar Clique. T'Challa is frequently alluded to by his innate title, the "Dark Jaguar." As one expert for the NSA has made sense of, being the Dark Puma is "similar to being Pope, President, and Top of the Joint Heads of Staff at the same time." T'Challa regularly wears a propensity that is both a strict frock and stately clothing of ancestral position.

Before the rise of the Wakandan country, spiritualist creatures known as Originators were ousted from the area by the people and the Orisha, the pantheon of Wakanda comprising Thoth, Ptah, Mujaji, Kokou, and Bast, the Jaguar Goddess.

In the far-off past, a huge shooting star comprised of the component vibranium crashed in Wakanda. The shooting star was named Mena Ngai. It was uncovered an age before the occasions of the current day. T'Challa, the ongoing Dark Puma, is the child of T'Chaka, the Dark Jaguar before him, and a relative of Bashenga.

Realizing that others would endeavor to control and rule Wakanda for this interesting and important asset, T'Chaka covers his country from the rest of the world. He auctions minute measures of the significant vibranium while secretly sending the nation's best researchers to concentrate abroad, subsequently transforming Wakanda into one of the world's most mechanically progressed countries.

In the end, notwithstanding, the pilgrim Ulysses Klaue tracks down his direction to Wakanda and conceals his work on a vibranium-controlled, sound-based weapon. When uncovered, Klaue kills T'Chaka, just to see his "sound blaster" turned on him by a lamenting teenage T'Challa. Klaue's right hand is obliterated, and he and his men escape.

Wakanda has a surprisingly high pace of change because of the hazardously mutagenic properties of the Vibranium Hill. An enormous number of these Wakandan Transforms are working for Erik Killmonger.

Vibranium radiation has saturated quite a bit of Wakanda's vegetation, including the Heart-Formed Spice eaten by individuals from the Dark Jaguar Clique (even though T'Challa once permitted a perishing Bug Man to eat it with the expectation that it would assist him with managing a baffling sickness) and the tissue of the White Gorilla eaten by the individuals from the White Gorilla Religion.

In the 2008 "Secret Attack" storyline, Skrull powers driven by Officer K'vvvr attack Wakanda and connect with Dark Puma and his powers. Because of weighty protection from the sending of innovative turns of events, the two sides are compelled to battle with swords and lances. The Wakandan powers deliberately wear puma covers; this keeps the Skrulls from zeroing in on assaults on their chief.

Despite misfortunes, the Wakandans rout the Skrulls. They kill each and everyone, including K'vvvr, and send their boat back, loaded with the bodies. An admonition against attacking Wakanda is left composed on the mass of the boat's control community.
While under the infinite force of the Phoenix Power, Namor assaults Wakanda for concealing the Vindicators and obliterates a large part of the country with a tsunami.

After the assault, all freaks (especially the individuals who were favoring Phoenix-controlled freaks) are restricted from entering Wakanda as expressed by Dark Jaguar. A few understudies from the Jean Dark school are gone after by the Wakandan public; the understudies scarcely escape with the assistance of Tempest.

At the point when Hydra controls a conscious infinite shape named Kobik into unconsciously supplanting the genuine Commander America's Steve Roger with his Hydra partner, then, at that point, institutes their Mysterious Domain, Wakanda is in danger to be taken over by the ascent of the psychological oppressor bunch across the universe, with its top dog T'Challa getting caught and compelled to give up, until all legends and a few reprobates who oppose Hydra at long last figure out how to get both Kobik and the genuine Steve Rogers back, while safeguarding both T'Challa and the remainder of both caught and controlled legends.

When Hydra's domain has been scattered, Wakanda extended its heritage to shape an intergalactic realm on Planet Bast, while additionally denying the freak boycott in their nation, for example, permitting Tempest to visit and help whenever.

The domain, presently including five worlds, emerges after a mission that looked for the beginning of Mena Ngai, the shooting star that brought the vibranium to Wakanda.

Chapter 2

Wakandan religion, White Gorilla, The Second Great War, Rule of S'Yan, Lion clique, Crocodile religion, Morlun, Language, Defenses, Social effect, (Inkolo yaseWakandan, iGorila emhlophe, iMfazwe eNkulu yesiBini, uLawulo lweS'Yan, iLion clique, inkolo yeeNgwenya, iMorlun, uLwimi, uKhuselo, impembelelo yeNtlalo.)

Wakanda contains a few strict organizations beginning from different spots in Africa, the Pantheon of Wakanda are known as The Orisha. Orisha is a Yoruba word significance soul or god. Bast the Jaguar Goddess, Thoth, lord of the moon and insight, and Ptah, the Shaper, are Heliopolitan divinities, who left old Egypt at the hour of the pharaohs. Kokou is a champion orisha from Benin.

Mujaji is a downpour goddess of the Lobedu nation of South Africa. Different divinities are venerated in Wakanda like Sekhmet and Sobek, other Helipolitan divinities, and the gorilla divine beings Ghekre and Ngi, revered by the Jabari clan.

The freak Ororo Munroe (otherwise known as Tempest), the ex of T'Challa and previous sovereign of Wakanda, is called Hadari-Yao ("Walker of Mists" in old Alkamite), a goddess who protects the equilibrium of normal things.

Bast the Jaguar Goddess, given Bast the antiquated Egyptian divinity, is the essential god of Wakanda. After the vibranium meteor fell, a few Wakandans were horrendously changed into "devil spirits" and started going after their kindred Wakandans.
T'Challa's progenitor Bashenga started to close the vibranium hill to outcasts. He shaped a strict request that watched the hill and battled to keep the "evil presence spirits" from spreading across the realm. As a stately and strict job, he took the title of Dark Jaguar as head of the Puma Clan. As a feature of the clique's services, a Dark Jaguar is qualified for the utilization of a heart-molded spice. The spice improves the actual characteristics of the individual who consumes it to approach godlike levels, likewise to the super-trooper serum.

White Gorilla
The White Gorilla Clique was an opponent gathering to the prevailing Jaguar Faction of Wakanda. Rather than adorning the Jaguar God, Bast, the White Gorilla Clique reveres the Chimp God, Ghekre. However the clique was banned by the remainder of Wakandan culture, the religion was as yet drilled by the Jabari Clan.

The Second Great War

During The Second Great War, the White Gorilla ignited with extreme contempt towards the Dark Puma and his kin. Probably acquiring his powers from a comparable supernatural custom as the one that engaged M'Baku years after the fact, the White Gorilla matched the Jaguar's actual ability, yet his town was no counterpart for the high-level African country.

The Gorilla held such disdain towards Dark Jaguars for not sharing their riches and assets that he consented to a union with the Nazis when the Red Skull and his powers wanted to attack the country to assume control over its inventory of Vibranium. He was essential for the power of Nazi supernatural people that attacked the Wakandan capital, going after the Imperial Royal residence of Wakanda before being crushed by Chief America.

Rule of S'Yan

A long time back, after the death of Ruler T'Chaka of Wakanda, his sibling S'Yan climbed to the privileged position and turned a major trend in Dark Jaguar. In a battling competition that was held like clockwork to permit the different clans of Wakanda the valuable chance to challenge the Dark Puma for the lofty position of Wakanda, the White Gorilla Clique entered a male warrior.

Nonetheless, the White Gorilla Religion's delegate was crushed by a soldier from the Lion Faction before he had an opportunity to challenge S'Yan for the high position. T'Chaka's child, T'Challa at last won the competition, turning a major trend into Dark Jaguar and leader of Wakanda.

The faction's most prominent champion, M'Baku, set to guarantee the high position of Wakanda while T'Challa was away from Wakanda for a considerable length of time. In the dismissal of the Wakandan orders, the White Gorilla Religion was re-established. M'Baku played out a custom to acquire upgraded strength by killing an uncommon white primate, washing in its blood, and eating its meat.

The clan that would turn into the Jabari adored Ngi, who was answerable for making Gorilla-Man. I depended on the Yaounde divinity of a similar name. At present, the Jabari clan loves the gorilla god Ghekre, in light of the Baoulé god of a similar name.

Wakanda developed from a tracker fighter society and was generally governed by its most prominent hero. The predominant Dark Puma

Religion prohibited the opponent White Gorilla Clique's love in Wakanda.

M'Baku (Man-Chimp) of the Jabari clan is quite possibly of Wakanda's most noteworthy fighters, second just to T'Challa, the Dark Puma himself. While T'Challa, lord of Wakanda, is on a multi-month time away from Wakanda, the aggressive M'Baku plots to usurp the high position. M'Baku spurns T'Challa's proclamations and restores the White Gorilla Religion, killing one of the uncommon white gorillas living in the wildernesses close to Wakanda. M'Baku washes in the gorilla's blood and eats its tissue which "magically" presents the gorilla's extraordinary strength upon M'Baku.

He attempts to overcome T'Challa in battle, wanting to assume control over the country but is beaten and expelled from Wakanda. As per the 2018 film, the White Gorilla clique referred to in the film as the Jabari (or the Mountain Clan), switches between the monkey god and Hanuman.

Lion clique

Sekhmet the Lion Goddess, in light of the divinity of a similar name, could have the type of any human admirers or the groups of those purified and forfeited her admirers, she changed these subjects into human symbols of herself. She has a few different abilities, some of which she has illustrated.

Sekhmet could fill in size, move at quick paces, transport herself as well as other people, and adjust her particular thickness. The Lion goddess had godlike strength and solidness, and she was everlasting. She can control the personalities of the powerless-willed.

Little is had some significant awareness of the historical backdrop of the Lion Goddess. She had lost numerous admirers over the years to the Faction of the Jaguar God, even though Sekhmet appeared before its adherents, and the Puma God just seems to its clerics.

Crocodile religion

The Crocodile Faction is an old religion of Wakanda that revered Sobek the "Crocodile god".

A long time back, after the death of Lord T'Chaka of Wakanda, his sibling S'Yan rose to the lofty position and turned the latest trend into Dark Puma. In a battling competition that was held like clockwork to permit the different clans of Wakanda the potential chance to challenge the Dark Jaguar for the high position of Wakanda, the Crocodile Religion entered a male soldier.

In any case, the Crocodile Clique's delegate was crushed by a warrior from the Lion Faction before he had an opportunity to challenge S'Yan for the privileged position. T'Chaka's child, T'Challa at last won the competition, turning the latest trend into Dark Jaguar and leader of Wakanda.

Morlun

In a little while, the Crocodile Religion revived Morlun with the goal that he could eat up the Dark Jaguar emblem and thusly debilitate the country of Wakanda. He right away turned on the Faction killing them all. In the beginning, Morlun benefited from the drawn-out Puma enemy Man-Primate. He was crushed by the latest Dark Jaguar Shuri, who, with the assistance of a witch specialist sent Morlun into limbo, where he had to fight the vast swarms of Death.

Sobek the Crocodile God, given the god of a similar name, has all the earmarks of being old and to some degree disregarded Wakandan god.

There are a few hypotheses about the historical background of Wakanda. The name might be propelled by a Siouan god called Wakanda, Wakonda, or Waconda; or WaWakandaa fictitious African clan from Edgar Rice Burroughs' clever The Alpha predator, written in 1915 however distributed post mortem in or the Kenyan Kamba ethnic gathering, likewise called Akamba or Wakamba; or "Kakinada which signifies "family" in Kikongo.

Language

In the comics, Wakanda has three authority dialects: Wakandan, Yoruba, and Hausa. In Wonder True to life Universe characters from Wakanda are depicted talking in the South African Xhosa language. The Jabari Clan misportrayed talking a vernacular like Igbo from Nigeria.

In the 2018 film Dark Jaguar, the Wakandan language is portrayed as being written in a Wakandan composing framework given the Nsibidi composing framework; the Wakandan composing framework was made for the film by creation fashioner Hannah Beachler.

Defenses

In the comics, Wakanda is the chief military power on Wonder Earth. The Wakandan Armed force is the country's fundamental ground power, while the Wakandan Naval force manages maritime activities. The Wakandan Air Watchman is the country's flying corps, which incorporates pilots wearing strong suits or battle shields. InTonsure harmony and strength in Wakanda, the Dark Jaguar picked Dora Milaje ("loved ones") from rival clans to act as his facial hair and formal spouses in-preparing.

Wakanda has a knowledge framework known as the N'Charu SilSliema spy network that worked across the globe to keep up with the country's mystery. It was viewed as great and positively better than the CIA an6. afterward, P.R.I.D.E. (Princess Official Knowledge Division Leaders) was created as the country's security organization. Wakanda is one of only a handful of exceptional Earth-616 civilizations that have alternate courses of action for managing Galactus, "The Devourer of Universes".

Social effect

In December 2019, it was found that the US Division of Horticulture's site recorded Wakanda as a deregulation accomplice, with a rundown of exchange merchandise that included ducks, jackasses, and dairy cows. The USDA guaranteed the made-up country had been added to the rundown "by accident during a staff test" and eliminated it not long after the general population became mindful of it.

The Wakandan capital city, Birnin Zana, could offer an option for what future urban communities could resemble in Africa. Currently, many brilliant city drives are being worked out in Africa, with numerous eco-urban communities converging across the mainland.

Senegalese-American vocalist Akon reported plans to fabricate "Akon City", a sunlight-based powered"real-life" Wakanda on 2,000 sections of land of waterfront land in Senegal propelled by Birnin Zana.

He originally shared his idea for a modern, mechanically progressed city in 2018 and said it would invite individuals from the African diaspora. The Washington Post detailed that the task had gotten $4 billion of the $6 billion venture important to construct Akon City.

Innovation journalists have likewise contrasted Wakandan standards with those communicated in African innovation research. Against pilgrims man-made intelligence, for instance, has been depicted as "with regards to Wakandan standards" by creating innovation for kind purposes. It additionally looks for "to stay away from algorithmic abuse and algorithmic mistreatment" in man-made brainpower.

The Wakanda name has likewise been taken on in private ventures. One model is Wakanda Spot, an African and multicultural bar in Adelaide, South Australia. Diversion at the bar incorporates DJs who play music from Africa and the African diaspora.
Wakanda, as portrayed in the 2018 film Dark Jaguar.

Wakanda shows up in media set in the Wonder Artistic Universe (MCU). Occupants from this rendition of the nation communicate in the Xhosa language, as T'Challa's entertainer Chadwick Boseman created utilizing a "local highlight in vying because of Wakanda would be. He did an incredible exploration of the exceptionally social parts of the person. DespitEven though an imaginary culture, [he figured] out ways of tying it into genuine African culture." Furthermore, it is situated at the northern finish of Lake Turkana, at a made-up point lining Ethiopia, South Sudan, Uganda, and Kenya.

In actuality, this region is a contested line locale known as the IElemiTriangle, guaranteed by every one of these nations. This follows the area of the country in the comic books as per Wonder Map book Shrugged.

The film Dark Jaguar further settled that, with regards to this guide area, it is a landlocked country in the focal mountains a long way from the coasts. Obstructed mountains and wildernesses around its boundaries have assisted Wakanda with disengaging itself from pariahs. Inside, Wakanda comprises lavish stream valleys, mountain

ranges wealthy in regular assets, and a fantastic capital city that coordinates space-age innovation with customary plans.
Wakanda comprises five clans, four of which are joined subject to the principal Dark Puma a long time back.

As in the comics, the four clans (The Stream clan, the Mining trTribethe Vendor clan, and the Boundary clan) love Bast, the puma god, among others, and have serious areas of strength for a practice of progenitor love.
The Stream Clan wears green garments produced using crocodile skin, for certain guys wearing a plate.
The Mining Clan aisin charge of the Vibranium that is mined, put away, and used.

The Dealer Clan is answerable for exchanges and specialties of workmanship, attire, and bits of craftsmanship. They likewise wear cloaks during marches to keep up with secrecy.
The Line Clan dwells on the rugged boundaries of Wakanda acting like ranchers to trick outsiders of Wakanda's abundance as well as their ability for reproducing white rhinoceros for reasons.

The fifth clan is the Jabari (or Mountain Clan) follows the White Gorilla faction of the god Hanuman and are resolute conservatives who confine themselves in the mountains. While thought about a piece of Wakanda, the Dark Jaguar's hold over the Jabari is shaky. During the film, their chief M'Baku rejects T'Challa as a commendable successor to the high position during his crowning ordinance and moves him to a stylized battle to guarantee it for himself. T'Challa wins the duel yet allows M'Baku to leave in harmony.

The rulers of every clan sit in the lord's chamber, and after the Mountain clan helps T,' Challa in his defeat of the usurper, Erik "Killmonger" Stevens, M'Baku has likewise conceded a seat on the committee in acknowledgment of his unwaveringly. The four fundamental clans talk in a reading edition of the Xhosa language while the Jabari talk in an Igbin o dialect.

The opening vivified succession to Dark Jaguar makes sense of Wakanda knew that the rest of the world was turning out to be progressively tumultuous all through different verifiable occasions that impacted Africa, for example, the Atlantic slave exchange, the colonization of Africa by European powers, The Second Great War, and The Second Great War.

The Dark Jaguars of the past, in any case, were given to shielding the name and didn't meddle, rather deciding to conceal Wakanda from the world - expecting that assuming they became involved and uncovered themselves, it would ultimately prompt outcasts attempting to attack Wakanda. All things being equal, Wakanda makes itself look like a little, unfortunate Underdeveloped country of humble herders, utilizing a high high-level graphic projection cover around its lines to conceal the high-level mechanical human progress inside.

A center strain of the film's story is the latest trend Dark Puma, T'Challa, is conflicted between his faithfulness to stow away and safeguard Wakanda as its top dog, and his still, small voice to help the vacillating scene past its lines. Later in the film, Killmonger shows up to attempt to hold onto the high position - sharing T'Challa's craving to end Wakanda's neutrality, however by overcoming the rest of the world utilizby ing Wakanda's cutting cutting-edge nations and weapons all things considered.

Eventually, T'Challa routs Killmonger and chooses to uncover Wakanda's real essence to the world during a location in the unified Countries. The film's prevalence prompted a pattern among competitors and superstars all over the planet to hurl "Wakanda Until the end of time" recon recognition of their triumphs. Chief Ryan Coogler expressed that his portrayal of Wakanda was roused by the southern African realm of Lesotho. Ba Sotho covers likewise turned out to be more known because of the film and its premise on Lesotho.

The following are Wakanda's included appearances:

Wakanda is momentarily displayed on a holographic guide in Iron Man 2, and is referenced in Justice fighters: Period of Ultron as the source country of vibranium, however, shows, up without precedent for the last scene of Commander America: Nationwide conflict, where Steve Rogers takes shelter with Bucky Barnes and to request the Wakandans' assistance in fixing Barnes Hydra programming. The film likewise acquaints Dark Puma with the MCU, in front of his performance film.

Wakanda's experience and culture are additionally extended in the previously mentioned performance film, which lays out that, as in the comics, the Dark Jaguar's godlike capacities come from consuming the "heart-molded spice", neighborhood vegetation that was transformed north of millions of years following openness to Vibranium.
In Justice fighters: Boundlessness War, individuals from the Vindicators travel to Wakanda with the expect expectation the nation's high high-levels can eliminate the Brain Stone from Vision without killing him.

At the point when the Outriders assault Wakanda, the Vindicators unite with the Wakandan armed force to battle them. Notwithstanding the guide's guidance, Rocket, and Groot, Thanos shows up in Wakanda and claims the Brain Stone, finishing the Endlessness Glove. He then, at that point, takes out a portion of the number of inhabitants known to mankind, including T'Challa and a few Wakandans, in an occasion later alluded to as the Blip.

In Vindicators: Final stage, Wakandan troops reestablished from the Blip rally behind T'Challa in Wakanda prior before through entryways to a war zone in upstate New York to battle the powers of Thanos.

Following the triumph in that fight, Wakanda commends the Blip's casualties' rebuilding.

In The Hawk and the Colder time of year Trooper (2021), Barnes has a flashback showing his recovery following his conditioning being scattered.
In What If...?, Wakanda is portrayed in various timetables; in the subsequent episode, T'Challa reunites with his family in Wakanda in the wake of having been erroneously kidnapped by Yondu Udonta and the Ravagers 20 years sooner. During the last snapshots of the fifth episode, Wakanda is shown, blockaded by zombies, and drove Thanos employing an almost complete Limitlessness Glove. In the 6th episode, Killmonger between Wakanda and the US and the latest into the end of Dark Puma. In the 10th episode, Shuri drives Pepper Potts and the Dora Milaje to capture Killmonger yet finds he vanished because of him having been enlisted by the Watcher to assist with battling a substitute Ultron.

Chapter3 :

The Progressive Force Of Dark Jaguar

The primary film I found in a venue had a dark legend. Lando Calrissian, played by Billy Dee Williams, had no superpowers, yet he ran his city. That film, the 1980 Star Wars continuation The Realm Strikes Back, presented Calrissian as a muddled person who made the best decision. That is one explanation I grew up realizing I could be something very similar.

Assuming you are understanding this and you are white, seeing individuals who appear as though you in broad communications most likely isn't something you contemplate frequently. Consistently, the way of life reflects you as well as almost limitless forms of you — leaders, writers, trash specialists, fighters, attendants, etc. The world shows you that your conceivable outcomes are endless. Presently, after a short reprieve, you again have a President.

We who are not white have significantly more difficulty not just tracking down portrayal of ourselves in broad communications and different fields of public life yet, in addition, finding portrayal that shows that our humankind is multifaceted. Connecting with characters onscreen is important not simply for us to feel seen and comprehended, yet in addition to other people who need to see and figure out us. At the point when it doesn't work out, we are the less fortunate for it.

This is one of the many reasons Dark Jaguar is critical. Seemingly simply one more section in an unending motorcade of superhero films is something a lot greater. It hasn't even hit theaters yet and its social impression is as of now colossal. It's a film about being dark in both America and Africa — and, all the more comprehensively, on the planet. As opposed to avoiding muddled subjects about race and personality, the film wrestles head-on with the issues influencing advanced dark life.

It is additionally unimaginably engaging, loaded up with opportune parody, pointedly arranged activity, and beautifully lit individuals, all things considered. "You have hero films that are abrasive dramatizations or activity comedies," chief Ryan Coogler says what time it is. Yet, this film, he says, handles another significant kind: "Superhuman movies that arrangement with issues of being of African plunge."

Dark Jaguar highlights tense activity groupings: "There was a point during the film when my sibling went to me and expressed out loud, 'Whatever will occur?'" Boseman says. "I saw him like, 'Simply watch the film!'"
Dark Jaguar is the eighteenth film in Wonder's True to life Universe, an establishment that has made $13.5 billion in the worldwide film industry throughout recent years. (Wonder is claimed by Disney.) It could be the first megabudget film about superheroes, yet about anybody to have an African-American chief and an overwhelmingly dark cast. Hollywood has never created a blockbuster this wonderfully dark.

The film, out Feb. 16, comes as the entertainment business is grappling with its poisonous treatment of ladies and people of variety. This quickly growing retribution one that mirrors the significance of portrayal in our way of life is extremely past due. Dark Jaguar is ready to demonstrate to Hollywood that African-American accounts can create benefits for all crowds. Also, more significantly, making motion pictures about people of color is important for showing that they matter.

The solicitation to the Dark Puma debut read "Regal clothing mentioned." Yet nobody made an appearance at the Dolby Theater on Hollywood Road on Jan. 29 seems to be an extra from an English outfit show. In plain view rather were crowns of an alternate sort rising head wraps made of different African textures. Oscar champ

Lupita Nyong'o wore her normal hair firmly wrapped over a shining bejeweled purple outfit.

Men, including stars Chadwick Boseman and Coogler, wore Afrocentric examples and dresses, dashikis, and boubous. Co-star Daniel Kaluuya, an Oscar chosen one for his star turn in getting Out, showed up wearing a kanzu, the proper tunic of his Ugandan heritage.

After the Obama period, maybe no part of this ought to feel pivotal. Yet, it does. During a backward social and political second energized to some degree by the white-nativist development, the actual presence of Dark Puma feels like an obstruction. Its topics challenge institutional inclination, its characters take unsubtle digs at oppressors, and its story remembers kaleidoscopic viewpoints of dark life and custom. The way that Dark Puma is magnificent just makes a difference.

Dark Jaguar Legend Rises

A while ago when the film was declared, in 2014, no one realize that it would be delivered into the laden environment of President Trump's America where a flourishing dark future appears to be more challenging to see. Trump's response to the Charlottesville confusion the previous summer likened those fighting prejudice with vicious neo-Nazis protecting a sculpture respecting a Confederate general.

Outsiders from Mexico, Focal America, and prevalently Muslim nations are a portion of the President's most continuous substitutes. So what's the significance here to see this film, a dream of outright dark greatness, in a second when the President supposedly, in a new gathering, excused the 54 countries of Africa as "sh-thole nations"?

As is common in the environment we're in, Dark Jaguar is as of now running into its portion of savages including a Facebook bunch that looked for, fruitlessly, to flood the survey aggregator Spoiled Tomatoes with negative evaluations of the film.

That Dark Jaguar means danger to some is obvious. A made-up African Ruler with the innovative conflict influence to obliterate you or, more regrettable, the abundance to purchase your property may not satisfy somebody who simply needs to consume the most recent Wonder section without more profound political thought.

Dark Puma is meaningful of the most useful reactions to extremism: as opposed to going for the hearts and psyches of bigots, it celebrates what the individuals who decide to restrict equivalent portrayal and privileges are overlooking, determinedly or not. They are passing up the full chance of the world and the very America they look to make "extraordinary." They can't stop this portrayal of it. While considering the people who prudently disdain Dark Puma and try to prevent it from affecting American culture, I reverberation the reaction that the film's legend T'Challa is known to give when cautioned of the individuals who try to attack his nation of origin: Let them an attempt.

The historical backdrop of dark power and the development that bore its name can be followed back to mid-year 1966. The lobbyist Stokely Carmichael was looking for more than simple freedom. As far as he might be concerned, coordination in a white-overwhelmed America implied digestion as a matter of course.

Around one year after the death of Malcolm X and the Watts riots in Los Angeles, Carmichael assumed control over the Understudy Nonviolent Planning Board of trustees from John Lewis. Carmichael chose to move the association away from a way of thinking of pacifism and raise the gathering's hostility to underline equipped self-protection, dark business possession, and local area control.

In June of that year, James Meredith, a dissident who four years sooner had turned into the primary individual of color who owned up to Ole Miss, began the Walk Against Dread, a long stroll of dissent from Memphis to Mississippi, alone. On the second day of the walk, he was injured by a shooter. Carmichael and a huge number of others went on in Meredith's nonappearance.

Carmichael, who was captured part of the way through the walk, was angered upon his delivery. "The main way we going to stop them, white men, from whuppin' us is to assume control over," he proclaimed before an enthusiastic group on June 16. "We been expressing opportunity for a long time and we ain't got nothin'. What we going to begin sayin' now is Dark Power!"

The dissident Stokely Carmichael, envisioned here at a 1966 meeting in Berkeley, Calif., stood firm against white persecution and promoted the term dark power
Dark Jaguar was brought into the world in the social liberties period, and he mirrored the governmental issues of that time. The month after Carmichael's Dark Power statement, the person appeared in Wonder Comics Awesome Four No. 52. Powerful strength and readiness were his fundamental elements, yet a virtuoso mind was his best characteristic.
"Dark Puma" wasn't a changed self-image; it was the proper title for T'Challa, Ruler of Wakanda, a made-up African country that, because of its elite hang on the sound-spongy metal vibranium, had turned into the most mechanically progressed country on the planet.

It was a dream of dark magnificence and, without a doubt, power in a difficult time, when over 41% of African Americans were at or underneath the neediness line and contained almost 33% of the country's poor.

Similar to the notorious Lieutenant Uhura character, played by Nichelle Nichols, that appeared in Star Trip in September 1966, Dark Puma was a declaration of Afrofuturism an ethos that wires African legends, innovation, and sci-fi and censures regular portrayals of (or, more terrible, endeavors to achieve) a future dispossessed of individuals of color.

His white makers, Stan Lee and Jack Kirby didn't intentionally invoke a dreamland reaction to Carmichael's call, yet the picture held power. T'Challa was not the area of strength for just taught; he was additionally sovereign. He didn't need to dominate. He was at that control point.

"You could say that this African country is the dream," says Boseman, who depicts T'Challa in the film. "However, to have the chance to pull from genuine thoughts, genuine spots, and genuine African ideas, and put it within this thought of Wakanda is an extraordinary chance to foster a feeling of what that character is, particularly when you're detached from it."

The person arose when the social liberties development legitimately started to expand requests of an America that had guaranteed so a lot and conveyed so little to its dark populace. 52 years after the presentation of T'Challa, those requests still can't seem to be completely replied to.

As per the Central bank, the commonplace African-American family had middle total assets of $17,600 in 2016. Interestingly, white families had middle total assets of $171,000. The progressive thing about Dark Puma is that it imagines a world not without prejudice but rather one in which individuals of color have the riches, innovation, and military could make everything fair a situation relevant not exclusively to the prevalently white scene of Hollywood at the same time, more significant, to the world in general.

The Dark Puma Party, the progressive association established in Oakland, Calif., a couple of months after T'Challa's presentation, was portrayed in the media as an undermining and extremist gathering with objectives that varied emphatically from the more radical vision of social equality pioneers like Martin Luther Ruler Jr. what's more, Lewis. Wonder even momentarily changed the person's name to Dark Panther as a result of the inescapable relationship with the Pumas, yet all the same, before long returned. For certain watchers, "Dark Jaguar" may have unmeritedly evil meanings, however, the 2018 film recovers the image to be commended by all as a symbol for change. The criticalness for change is part of the way the thing Carmichael was attempting to communicate in the mid-year of '66, and the people pulling the strings expected to tune in. It's obvious in 2018.

Moviegoers originally experienced Boseman's T'Challa in Wonder's 2016 gathering hit Chief America: Nationwide conflict, and he quickly cut a striking figure in his smooth vibranium suit. As Dark Jaguar opens, with T'Challa lamenting the demise of his dad and understanding his unexpected rising to the Wakandan lofty position, obviously our legend's regal childhood has kept him shielded from the real factors of how foundational prejudice has contacted pretty much every dark life across the globe.

The comic, particularly in its latest manifestations as delivered by the scholars Ta-Nehisi Coates and Roxane Gay, has attempted to erase Eurocentric misguided judgments of Africa — and the film's symbolism and topical material go with the same pattern. "Individuals frequently ask, 'What is Dark Puma? What is his power?' And they have a misguided judgment that he just has power through his suit," says Boseman. "The person is existing with power inside power."

Coogler says that Dark Jaguar, similar to his past movies — including the police-fierceness show Fruitvale Station and his imaginative Rough continuation Ideology — investigates issues of character. "That is something I've generally battled with personally," says the chief. "Like whenever that I first figured out I was dark." He's discussing epidermal mindfulness than figuring out how white society sees his dark skin. "Character, yet names. 'Who are you?' is an inquiry that surfaces a great deal in this film. T'Challa knows precisely what his identity is. The main bad guy in this film has many names."

That lowlife comes as Erik "Killmonger" Stevens, a previous dark operations fighter with Wakandan ties who tries to both outmaneuver and pound T'Challa for the crown. As played by a scene-stealing Michael B. Jordan, Killmonger's inspirations enlighten prickly inquiries regarding how individuals of color overall ought to best utilize their power.

In the film, Killmonger is, as Coogler, a local of Oakland. By investigating the unique encounters of Africans and African Americans, Coogler focuses a brilliant light on the mystic scars of subjection's heritage and how dark Americans persevere through its genuine results of it in the current day. Killmonger's viewpoint is delivered in full; his fury over how he and other individuals of color across the world have been disappointed and debilitated is reasonable.

Coogler, who co-composed the screenplay with Joe Robert Cole, likewise incorporates one more significant adversary from the comics: the obnoxious and extremist Ulysses Klaue (Andy Serkis). "What I love about this experience is that it might have been dark double-dealing:

he will battle Klaue, he will pursue the white man and that is all there is to it — that is the adversary,"
Boseman says. He perceives that a few fans will disagree with a dark male miscreant battling dark heroes. Killmonger battles T'Challa as well as fighter ladies like the covert agent Nakia (Nyong'o), Okoye (Danai Gurira), and the remainder of the Dora Milaje, T'Challa's all-female illustrious gatekeepers. Killmonger and Shuri (Letitia Wright), T'Challa's quippy tech-virtuoso sister, additionally go head to head.

T'Challa and Killmonger are identical representations, isolated exclusively by the mishap of where they were conceived. "What they don't understand," Boseman says, "is that the best struggle you will at any point face will be the contention with yourself."

Both T'Challa and Killmonger must be convincing for the film to succeed. "The superhuman is who places you in the seat," Coogler says.
"That is who you need to see proof to be the best. However, I'll be doomed on the off chance that the miscreants ain't cool as well. They must have the option to confront the legend, and make them say, 'Man, I couldn't say whether the legend will get.'"
"On the off chance that you don't have that," Boseman says, "you don't have a film."

On set, Coogler works with star Gurira. "Dark Puma is about a person who works with his family and is liable for an entire country," he says. "That obligation doesn't switch off."
This isn't simply a film about a dark superhuman; it's a lot of a dark film. It conveys a weight that neither Thor nor Chief America could lift: serving a dark crowd that has a distant memory underrepresented.

For such a long time, films that portray a reality where whiteness isn't the default have been ghettoized, showcased generally to crowds of variety as specialty diversion, rather than as a component of the standard.

Consider Tyler Perry's Madea films, Malcolm D. Lee's unexpected 1999 hit The Best Man, or the Barbershop establishment that was sent off in 2002. Be that as it may, throughout the last year, the progress of movies including Getting Out and Young ladies Excursion have done significantly greater business in the cinematic world, prompted business recognition, and printed new stars like Kaluuya and Tiffany Haddish.

Those two hits have just supported a contention that has endured for a long time before Spike Lee made his introduction: dark movies with dark subjects and dark stars can and ought to be showcased like some other. Nobody discusses Woody Allen and Wes Anderson motion pictures as "white films" to be showcased just to that crowd.

Dark Puma denotes the greatest move yet in this wave: it's both a dark film and the freshest contestant in the most bankable film establishment ever. For a vigilant and risk-disinclined film business, driven to a great extent by white film chiefs who have been generally inclined toward greenlight projects highlighting characters who seem as though them, Dark Jaguar will offer verification that a portrayal of truth of some different option from whiteness can make a lot of cash.

A portion of the film's initial achievement can be credited to Nate Moore, an African-American chief maker in Wonder's film division who has been vocal about the significance of remembering dark characters for the Wonder universe. However, past Wakanda, the inquiries of force and obligation, it appears, are not just relevant to the characters in Dark Puma. When this film passes the entryways over, true to form, Hollywood should accomplish other things to deal with that issue than only greenlight more dark stories. It likewise needs more Nate Moores.

"I know individuals [in the diversion industry] will see this and try to it," Boseman says. "In any case, this is likewise having individuals inside spaces — watchman positions, individuals who can open entryways and take that thought. How might this be finished? How might we be addressed optimistically?"

Since Dark Puma checks such an exceptional second the energy for the film feels practically motor. Dark Jaguar parties are being coordinated, pre-and post-film soirées for fans new and old. A video of youthful Atlanta understudies moving into their homeroom once they learned they planned to see the film together became famous online toward the beginning of February.

Oscar champ Octavia Spencer declared on her Instagram account that she'll be in Mississippi when Dark Jaguar opens and that she intends to purchase out a theater "in an underserved local area there to guarantee that all our earthy colored kids can see themselves as a superhuman."

Numerous social liberties pioneers and other exploring progenitors have gotten luxurious realistic medicines, in films including Malcolm X, Selma, and Secret Figures. Jackie Robinson even depicted himself onscreen. Fictitious celluloid bosses have included Virgil Tibbs, John Shaft, and Saucy Brown. Lando, as well. Be that as it may, Dark Puma matters more since he is our most obvious opportunity so that individuals of every variety might be able to see a dark legend. That is all there is to it sort of force.

We didn't make it two stages into the cinema's front entryway before we were welcomed, "What's great, my brothas?" As he yelled to us over the majority in the ticket line, he folded his arms, gripped his clenched hands, and gave a slight bow — a Wakandan welcoming.

"Ya will comprehend after you watch it," he said. Also, with that, he vanished into the evening, and we entered Wakanda.

In general, I loved Wonder's new blockbuster, Dark Puma. It wasn't "the most ideal film I have at any point seen," as one individual let me know more than once in the lobby, however it was one of the better Wonder films. The story gets after the blast in a past Wonder film where T'Chaka, the lord of Wakanda, bites the dust in the bombarding. T'Challa, his child, then gets back to his country to accept the lofty position and assume his legitimate position as lord of Wakanda and as the Dark Jaguar. Be that as it may, resistance emerges, leaving the destiny of Wakanda — and the remainder of the world.

Having watched a social equality narrative in advance, I tracked down the philosophies of the two principal characters to thought-incite. Furthermore, albeit Dark Jaguar has great activity scenes, solid characters, a fair story, and supportive inquiries concerning worldwide obligation, the charm of the film for some blacks in the theater was not, in that frame of mind, about the legend essentially, yet about the general public. I left needing to resemble the Dark Puma. Yet, I left needing to be in Wakanda significantly more.

Over a Film

In the film, Wakanda is a made-up African country stowed away from the remainder of the world. It is uncolonized, mechanically progressed, overflowing with dark greatness and magnificence, productive, hilly, and stunning. In any case, the perfect world itself, not the dark superhuman, hit an old throb that 400 years in America hasn't verged on calming. We unite behind superheroes like the Dark Jaguar since we trust that they can lead us to Wakanda.

"We lift superheroes like the Dark Jaguar since we trust that they can lead us to Wakanda."
However, such a spot was pretended. Or on the other hand, so I thought.

Indeed, even before I could watch the film, I heard the stream of Wakanda's cascade, felt the daylight of her happiness, and saw her kin dance to her music. Everyone was wearing African clothing. Families fixed up to take pictures with the Dark Jaguar banner. Outsiders welcomed each other in the lobbies. The film, too much, was more than a film. It turned into a cut of Wakanda.

We strolled shortly before kickoff and individuals were at that point situated. What's more, we were all early, not because we needed to get great seats (they were at that point relegated), but since we would have rather not missed a second. We needed to be in Wakanda as far as might be feasible. For three hours, we celebrated equality, pioneers who thought often profoundly about the African American population, and the excellence of dark culture freed from its set of experiences and current battles.

As my Sierra Leonean Christian sibling and I stayed there, we stood amazed at the particular joy we felt in this larger part of dark social them. This film was to a great extent for ourselves and by us (as it were), and it envisioned a world large numbers of us have longed for quite a long time, a world a considerable lot of us would pick over this world in a second.

And yet, as a Christian, I thought, "What of the magnificence of variety? Shouldn't so be the ideal? Is it off-base to feel so comfortable in Wakanda?"

Clan of the Jaguar

The comparability is quite possibly of Eden's best organic product. If Adam might have murmured in heaven, it would have been in naming the creatures without having the option to find "a partner fit for him" (Beginning 2:20). The distinction in the turtle's shell satisfied, the polish of the falcon's taking off enamored, however, these were not Eve. Furthermore, when Adam's eager eyes began to diminish, God brought her from himself — and she caught him in manners no other animal could. So magnificently unique, but, at long last, "bone of my bones and tissue of my tissue" (Beginning 2:23).

"A homogeneous society, a clan of the Jaguar, gave an unmistakable delight to those inside it."

This great time equivalence is what C.S. Lewis refers to as the start of companionship: "The common articulation of opening Fellowship could be something like, 'What? You as well? I assumed I was the one to focus on" (The Four Loves, 65). Fellowship shares a typical love — or trouble — that others don't share. I got a Wakandan gathering at the cinema since I encountered being dark in America. I and the other individuals of color in the theater understood what it is to be racially profiled, to be the "one to focus on" in pretty much every setting, and to live under the ongoing administration — we understood what it is to live beyond Wakanda.

Thus, we stayed there with many individuals who seemed as though us and snickered at jokes that were stowed away from some beyond the way of life. We watched individuals who seemed as though us on the screen battle for the issues of individuals in a la la land where our networks prospered. No bondage. No Jim Crow South. No below-average citizenship. No making sense of what that expression implies — we as a whole knew. A homogeneous society, a clan of the Jaguar, gave an unmistakable delight to those inside it.

The Approaching Wakanda

I can recollect the primary Wakandan experience I had with Christians. I can in any case recollect the excitement of strolling in to see a room loaded with African and African-American Christians ablaze for Jesus. Never had I encountered anything like it. People from comparative foundations, who talked in similar vernacular, opened up their Books of scriptures to hear from and love God.
Furthermore, during that time, I found that Paul recognized the delights of comparability, particularly for those external the confidence: to the Jews, he turned into a Jew, to those under the law

as one under the law; he turned into everything to all individuals to win nearly (1 Corinthians 9:19-23). Winding up in a room brimming with comparable individuals can cause you to feel comfortable like little else can. However, as I went on in my Christian walk, Paul instructed me that there is a joy that surpasses even the pleasantness of social equality.

"The solid church is a preview of the approaching heaven where Jesus joins a group of contrasts."
He talked about the culmination of bliss that comes from the different churches in Philippi — brimming with men, ladies, kids, minimal Jewish young ladies, and Roman guards — staying in dauntless solidarity together (Philippians 2:2). He talked about the greatness of Jesus spilling his blood to join his multiethnic individuals together into one new man (Ephesians 2:15). John added to the discussion by showing me a page from the last section of every devotee's story:

After this I looked, and see, an extraordinarily large number that nobody could number, from each country, from all clans and people groups and dialects, remaining before the lofty position and before the Sheep, dressed in white robes, with palm branches in their grasp, and shouting out with a boisterous voice, "Salvation has a place with our God who sits on the privileged position, and to the Sheep!"
(Det.7:9-10)
In God's promise, I discovered that Wakanda has borders that grow past social likeness. All countries, all clans, and all tongues share normal citizenship, a never-ending partnership that joins permanently. Furthermore, this reality has proactively started.

In Christ, I can welcome a young person in the mountains of Guatemala as "my sibling." I can disclose my most profound torments to an old white lady as I request that she petition God for me. Hitched collective with singles; the rich eat with poor people. The sound church is a preview of the approaching heaven where Jesus, our Ruler, joins a group of contrasts. Our qualifications don't vanish, however, a more noteworthy justification for solidarity shows up. This family is associated with better blood: his.

In God's coming Wakanda, he offers something much more prominent than the universe of Dark Puma: solidarity made wonderful through variety. The various varieties will finish the canvas. The various notes will strike harmony. The eye will get together with the nose and the arm to restore the body. There, association — not consistency — will be the more prominent light. There, the transitory fellowship of the Puma will be immersed in the different and timeless unity of the Sheep.

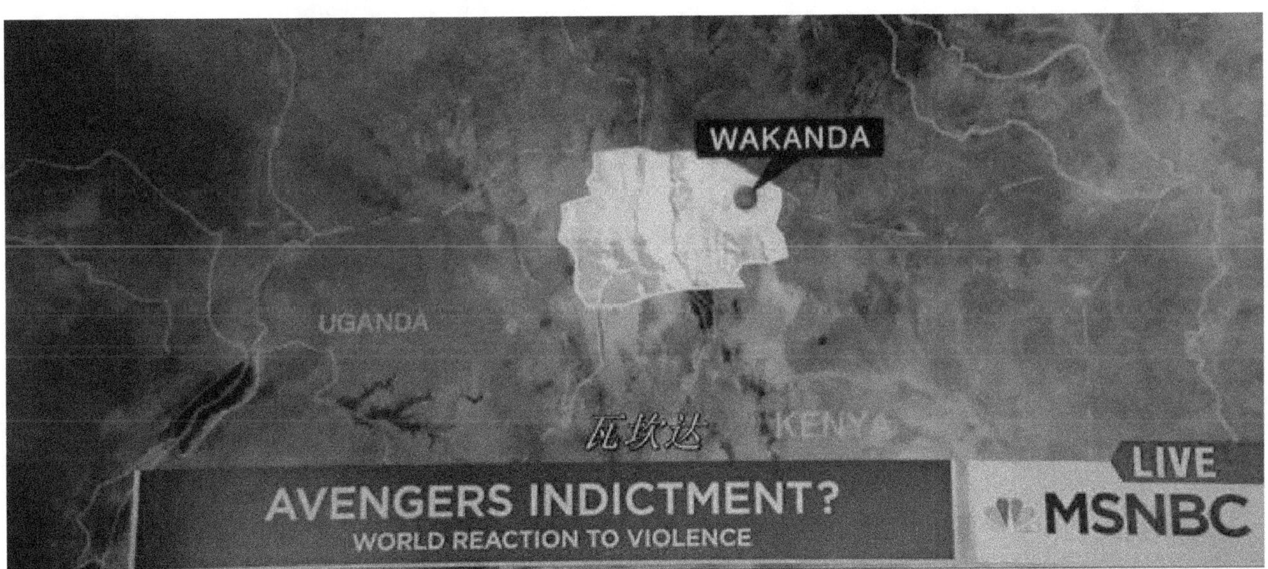

www.ingramcontent.com/pod-product-compliance
Lightning Source LLC
LaVergne TN
LVHW080559160826
845677LV00010B/1911
9798356150289